ANIMALS AROUND THE WORLD

ALL ABOUT
NORTH AMERICAN
HAWAIIAN MONK SEALS

Lisa Petrillo

EZ READERS

Creating Young Nonfiction Readers

EZ Readers lets children delve into nonfiction at beginning reading levels. Young readers are introduced to new concepts, facts, ideas, and vocabulary.

Tips for Reading Nonfiction with Beginning Readers

Talk about Nonfiction
Begin by explaining that nonfiction books give us information that is true. The book will be organized around a specific topic or idea, and we may learn new facts through reading.

Look at the Parts
Most nonfiction books have helpful features. Our *EZ Readers* include a Contents page, an index, and color photographs. Share the purpose of these features with your reader.

Contents
Located at the front of a book, the Contents displays a list of the big ideas within the book and where to find them.

Index
An index is an alphabetical list of topics and the page numbers where they are found.

Glossary
Located at the back of the book, a glossary contains key words/phrases that are related to the topic.

Photos/Charts
A lot of information can be found by "reading" the charts and photos found within nonfiction text. Help your reader learn more about the different ways information can be displayed.

With a little help and guidance about reading nonfiction, you can feel good about introducing a young reader to the world of *EZ Readers* nonfiction books.

Mitchell Lane

PUBLISHERS

2001 SW 31st Avenue
Hallandale, FL 33009
www.mitchelllanepub.com

First Edition, 2025.

Author: Lisa Petrillo
Designer: Ed Morgan
Editor: Sharon F. Doorasamy

Names/credits:
Title: All About North American Hawaiian Monk Seals
by Lisa Petrillo
Description: Hallandale, FL :
Mitchell Lane Publishers, [2025]

Series: Animals Around the World
Library bound ISBN: 9781680204216
eBook ISBN: 9781680204223
Paperback ISBN: 979-8-89260-137-5

EZ readers is an imprint of Mitchell Lane Publishers

Library of Congress Cataloging-in-Publication Data
Names: Petrillo, Lisa, author.
Title: All about North American Hawaiian monk seals
by Lisa Petrillo.
Description: First edition. | Hallandale, FL : EZ Reade
an imprint of Mitchell Lane Publishers, 2020. | Serie
Animals around the world-North American animals
Includes bibliographical references and index.
Identifiers: LCCN 2018030966| ISBN 9781680204216
(library bound) | ISBN 9781680204223 (ebook)
Subjects: LCSH: Hawaiian monk seal—Juvenile
literature.
Classification: LCC QL737.P64 P465 2020 |
DDC 599.79/2—dc23
LC record available at https://lccn.loc.gov/20180309

Photo credits: Freepik.com, Shutterstock, p. 20-21
©Mike Pitts/naturepl.com, mapchart.net

CONTENTS

The Hawaiian monk seal lives off the coast of Hawaii. They are **rare**.

Hawaiian monk seals are amazing **divers**. They zip through the ocean.

Monk seals look cute. Their skin folds around their necks. This skin looks like the robes **monks** wear. This is why they are called monk seals.

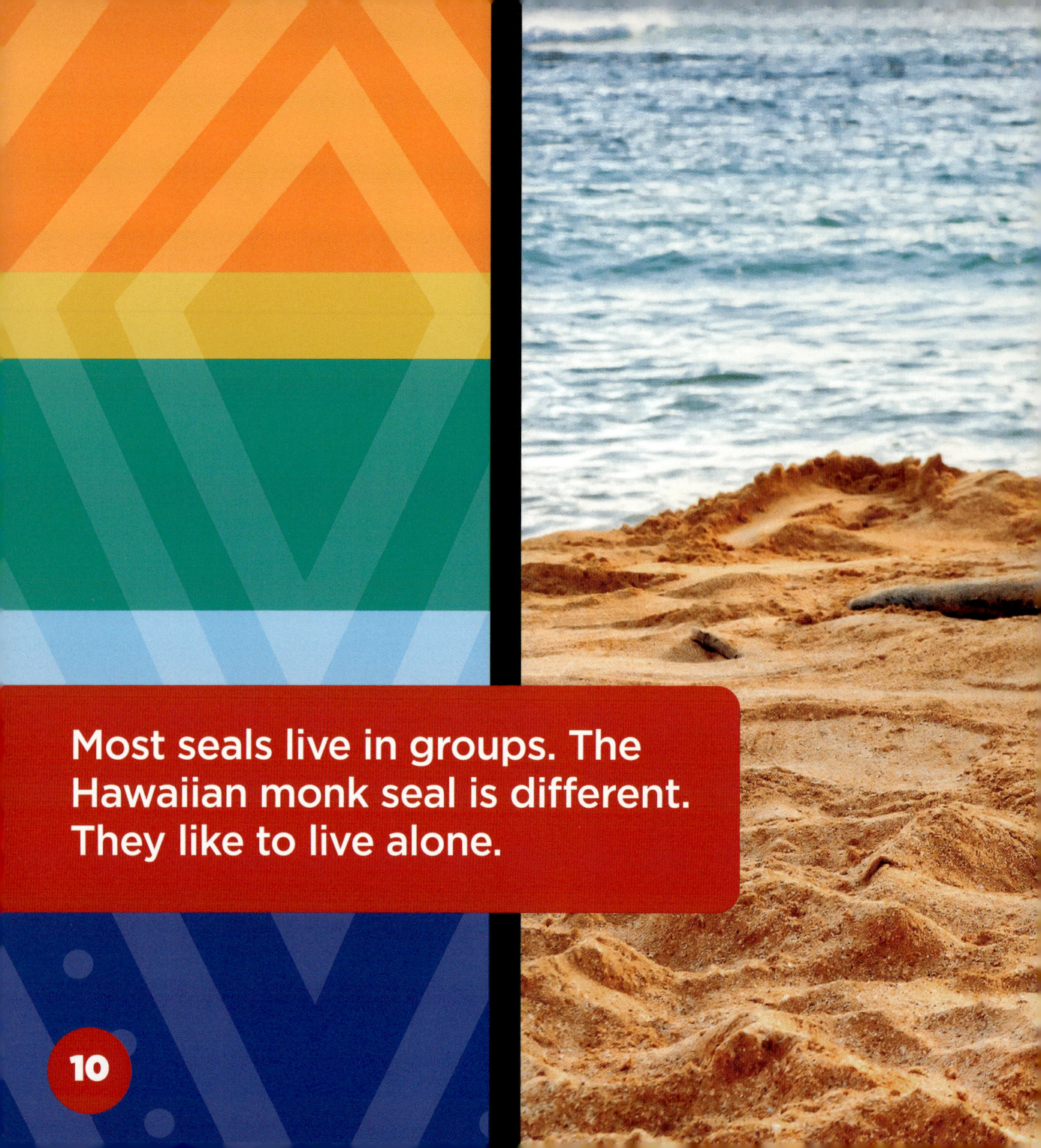

Most seals live in groups. The Hawaiian monk seal is different. They like to live alone.

Hawaiian monk seals have gray backs. Their bellies are silver gray. They grow long and plump.

13

The Hawaiian monk seal eats fish, eels, and octopus. They dive deep for food. This is a special talent.

Baby seals are called **pups**. Pups are born with fuzzy black fur. Their coat sheds into gray sealskin.

Pups swim right from birth. Their mothers teach them.

19

People hunt monk seals. They leave trash in their waters too. Many people are trying to help save monk seals.

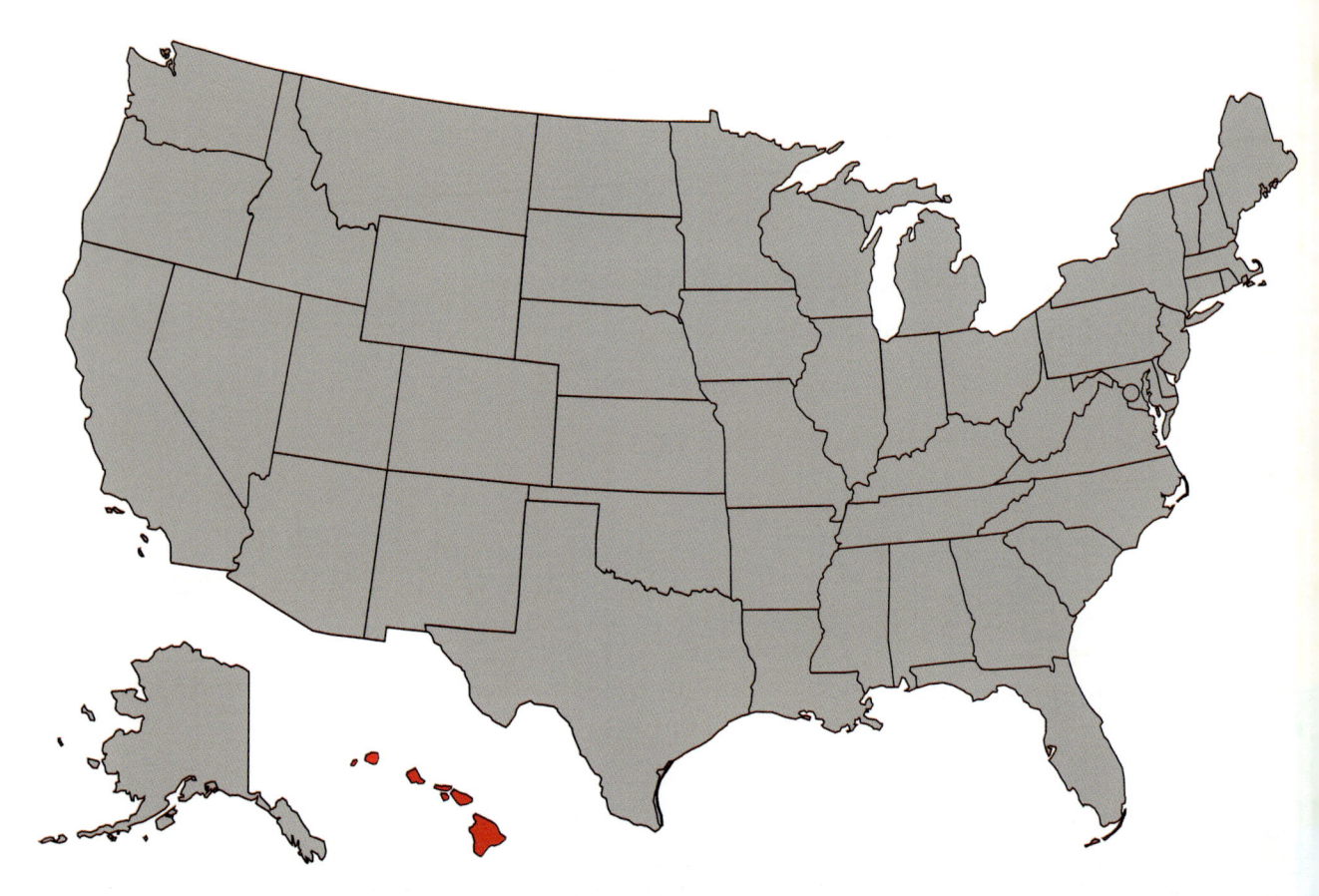

WHERE DO HAWAIIAN MONK SEALS LIVE?

Hawaiian monk seals live in the Hawaiian islands. The islands are west of the California coast in the Pacific Ocean.

22

INTERESTING FACTS

- The Hawaiian monk seal eats at night and sunbathes during the day.
- Monk seals dive down to find a spiny lobster, then slap it on the surface to break it open.
- Pups stay with their mothers for five to seven weeks.
- Monk seals grow to be full-sized by age four and have babies around age five.
- The monk seal is the only **mammal** native to Hawaii.
- Monk seals shed their skin each year.

PARTS OF A HAWAIIAN MONK SEAL

Flippers
Side flippers at about shoulder height help the Hawaiian monk seal steer and power through water at amazing depths.

Tail
Fins at the tail end of a monk seal give it great power.

Whiskers
They have black whiskers at the end of their noses like dogs.

Ears
The monk seal has no ears on the outside. It has ear canals on the inside of its head that allow it to hear.

GLOSSARY

diver
A person or animal that jumps into the water

mammal
A warm-blooded animal that breathes air, has a backbone, and drinks its mother's milk when a baby

monk
A man who is a member of a religious group and lives a simple life in quiet places

pups
Babies of Hawaiian monk seals, usually one born per mother

rare
Not often seen or found

FURTHER READING

Harvey, Jeanne Walker. *Honey Girl: The Hawaiian Monk Seal*. Mount Pleasant, SC: Arbordale Publishing, 2017.

Allen, Kevin. "5 Things About the Hawaiian Monk Seal You Need To Know." *Hawaii Magazine*, August 9, 2017. https://www.hawaiimagazine.com/content/5-things-about-hawaiian-monk-seal-you-need-know.

ON THE INTERNET

Marine Mammal Center
http://www.marinemammalcenter.org/education/marine-mammal-information/pinnipeds/hawaiian-monk-seal/

National Geographic Critter Cam: Hawaiian Monk Seal
https://video.nationalgeographic.com/video/wd-ep7-monkseal

National Oceanic and Atmospheric Administration: Hawaiian Monk Seal
https://www.fisheries.noaa.gov/species/hawaiian-monk-seal

INDEX